SOLVING VIOLENCE PROBLEMS IN YOUR SCHOOL

Why a Systematic Approach is Necessary

A Guide for Educators

Carole Remboldt

JOHNSON INSTITUTE

HAZELDEN®

Acknowledgment

The content of this booklet is based on the violence intervention and prevention model originally developed by Carole Remboldt for the Johnson Institute.

Solving Violence Problems in Your School
Why a Systematic Approach is Necessary
A Guide for Educators

Hazelden Information and Educational Services
Center City, Minnesota 55012-0176
1-800-328-9000 (Toll Free U.S., Canada, and
the Virgin Islands)
1-651-213-4000 (Outside the U.S. and Canada)
1-651-213-4590 (24-hour Fax)
www.hazelden.org

ISBN 1-56246-095-1

Cover and page design: Daniel Crombie
Printed in the United States of America

Table of Contents

Introduction

Far too many of our children live in fear of violence at school. It's not surprising that the constant threat of violence has a devastating effect on their psychological well-being and their ability to function and learn in a school environment. Research indicates that children who attend schools where violence is prevalent are less likely to succeed because their fear of physical harm makes it difficult to concentrate on learning. At the same time, children who are not successful in school are more likely to be violent than those who are succeeding, thus perpetuating the violence.

According to Deborah Prothrow-Stith, M.D., assistant dean of the Harvard School of Public Health and an expert on teenage violence, "Learning itself is a vital form of violence prevention. The cognitive skills children slowly develop during years of studying English, social studies, math, and science help them to reason their way through stressful and dangerous situations. When children have well-developed language and analytic skills, they are more likely to think before striking and use words instead of force to persuade."[1]

The American Psychological Association (APA), too, recognizes a link between aggressiveness and poor school achievement. In a summary report of the APA's Commission on Violence and Youth, the commission writes, "In early childhood, aggressive and disruptive classroom behavior contributes to poor school achievement and poor peer relations. In addition to academic failure contributing to later antisocial behavior, it now seems that early antisocial and aggressive behavior patterns learned at home and elsewhere also may interfere with school learning and with the development of positive peer relations in the school context."[2]

Although some educators are alarmed at the explosion of violence in their schools, others either deny that a problem exists or believe it isn't really as bad as everyone says.

Is Violence Really a Problem in Schools?

In 1993, 65,000 students in grades 6 through 12 responded to a national survey on violence in schools. The results were alarming:

- 37 percent of students do not feel safe in school (nearly double the number compared with a similar survey conducted in 1989).

- 50 percent know someone who switched schools to feel safer.

- 43 percent avoid school restrooms.

- 20 percent avoid hallways.

- 45 percent avoid school grounds.

- 26 percent of the girls and 49 percent of the boys reported being physically assaulted.

- 67 percent of students say that school lockers are not a safe place for valuables.

- 22 percent have been robbed of an item worth more than $10.

- 55 percent of students in grades 10 through 12 say they know that weapons are in their school.

- 79 percent of students say violence is often caused by "stupid things like bumping into someone."

- 47 percent say teachers spend half of their class time disciplining students.

- 63 percent say they'd learn more if they felt safer in school.

- 81 percent say they would be happier in general if they felt safer in school.[3]

The survey's findings mirror other available national data on school violence. The National Education Association reports that:

- Every hour of every school day, 2,000 students are physically attacked on school grounds.

- Each school day 160,000 students skip classes because they fear physical harm.

- One in five students regularly carries a weapon to school (one in 20 carries a gun).

- Each school day, more than 6,000 teachers are threatened with injury and 260 are assaulted.

- 25 percent of big city public schools now have metal detectors.

But violence is not just a problem in big city schools. Violent outbursts among students and between students and teachers are increasing not only in urban and suburban schools, but in smaller rural schools as well. A National School Boards Association survey found that 43 percent of rural school administrators say violence in their schools has increased from five years ago.

A Lou Harris survey, released in July 1993, found that 40 percent of urban, 36 percent of suburban, and 43 percent of rural teenagers personally knew someone who had been killed or injured by gunfire. Many educators and parents have awakened to the realization that violence by and against young people is a growing national problem that cuts across geographic, economic, and racial boundaries and is threatening the very fabric of our nation's schools.

What is Causing Violence in the Schools?

What appears to be happening, as the data suggests, is that anger and aggression are erupting in children and adolescents today with unprecedented intensity and frequency. In the past, angry conflicts among young people may have resulted in some pushing, shoving, maybe a few punches, or a heated verbal exchange. Today, it is not unusual for them to express their anger or resolve conflicts by threatening to use, or actually using, dangerous weapons to "win an argument" or "save face."

Some experts believe that because violence has become an accepted norm in the media, children have actually become "desensitized" to the level of violence around them. Television and films consistently portray the "good guys" as well as the "bad guys" using violence as a matter of course to solve problems quickly and effectively. The prime messages children get from these portrayals is that good guys use violence as a first resort, and any number of violent acts is okay because the end justifies the means. These messages also imply that violence doesn't really cause lasting injury, at least not in the movies or on TV. The heroes always seem to escape to return unscathed for the next scene, episode, or sequel.

Other experts believe that youth violence is rooted in the social and economic changes that have swept the country over the last two decades. Financial pressures and fast-paced careers have contributed to parents spending more hours on the job and fewer hours with their children.

From a national sample of nearly 50,000 sixth through twelfth graders responding to the Johnson Institute *StudentView*® Survey, more than one in three (36.4 percent) said they never or hardly ever talked to their fathers about problems or questions; 16.3 percent said they never or hardly ever talked with their mothers.

We know that many parents unwittingly teach their children by example to act violently; too many parents are so frustrated, overworked, financially stretched, and worried that they have little time to stop and calmly address the needs of their children. Parents often exemplify violence to their children by exploding at them, yelling at them, or being physically, emotionally, or sexually abusive. As a consequence, many of today's children are not learning how to appropriately handle their anger by using words to talk it out. Instead, they use their fists, feet, or weapons.

Many young people don't know how to walk away from an argument or fight. They don't know how to back off, cool down, and take time to sort out what's really wrong; they don't know how to negotiate or compromise to resolve conflicts with others. Many young people apparently only know how to react—quickly, violently, and without forethought.

Add to this mix an increasingly violent society where violent behavior is often depicted as glamorous, exciting, and the pathway to power, and it's not difficult to see why so many young people have learned to use violence as a normal and viable way to solve problems or get what they want. Young people also often see many of their peers use violence to their advantage at home, at school, or on the streets with only shallow protests or warnings from parents or other adults, including teachers. This is called the *disinhibition* of children to violent behavior. This disinhibition has created a terrible problem for schools and placed enormous pressure on educators to do something to solve the problem.

Why Haven't Violence Prevention Programs Seemed to Work?

Because it is logical to assume that a problem such as violence cannot be solved unless its causes are identified and understood, heated debates rage on among concerned adults as to who or what is to blame. The truth is that violence is so complex, widespread, and deeply rooted in our culture and has so many different forms—domestic or family violence, acquaintance violence, random violence, to name a few—that it may be many years before a complete and coherent explanation of the causes of violence is within our reach. Nevertheless, because of the pressure being put on schools to do something to stop the escalating violent behavior among students, and between students and teachers, some schools have already attempted to develop strategies and implement programs to prevent and combat violence—but without much success.

For example, according to U.S. House of Representatives Bill 4535, which introduced the "Classroom Safety Act of 1992," 25 percent of major school districts currently use metal detectors to prevent weapons from entering the schools. But there is little evidence that metal detectors are effective in reducing the number of violent incidents on school campuses. The National School Safety Center states that metal detectors have had little effect. And a survey of ninth through twelfth graders attending New York City public schools suggests that school districts may even be throwing their money away.[4]

Other militant attempts to combat violence in schools such as hiring armed security guards, conducting routine locker searches, and placing cameras on buses have been well-intentioned, but relatively ineffective at preventing violence. Often these measures only serve to drive the problem underground, leaving students and teachers even more vulnerable after school or outside school grounds.

Other strategies to prevent violence problems in schools, such as implementing special educational curricula or providing students with training in anger management, conflict resolution, and peer mediation, while necessary and beneficial for most students, have failed to produce the hoped-for results. Why haven't these attempts to solve violence problems in schools seemed to work? While most of these single "get tough" or "get smart" responses by educators have had some short-term success and have had the support of most parents and other concerned adults, the responses have not proved successful in the long run for the following reasons:

- Often they are simplistic or piecemeal responses addressing only one or two aspects of a multi-faceted problem.

- They tend to create a militant or punitive atmosphere that punishes all students through overly restrictive policies and procedures (metal detectors, locker sweeps, and the like), thus losing students' respect and cooperation.

- They breed feelings of fear, anxiety, suspicion, and mistrust rather than feelings of safety, security, and support.

- They tend to drive violent behavior "underground" or outside the school where students and teachers are more vulnerable.

- They often attempt to remove the "problem" (in other words, the "bad kids") from the school, creating the impression that only "bad kids" are involved in violent behavior.

- They tend to deal with all incidents of violence in schools as "criminal issues" when most incidents of violence are really "behavioral health" issues.

- They are almost invariably "student-centered" responses, implying that young people are solely responsible for violence problems in schools.

Perhaps the primary reason these responses have proved ineffective is that the problem of violence requires a response that addresses and engages *the entire school system*, children and adults, as well as the other major systems of which young people are a part—families and the community.

Our search for the reasons why individual school-based programs and strategies to prevent and combat violence have not worked has provided some positive and encouraging insights. For one thing, the search revealed the widespread and deep-seated concern and dedication of many educators and other professionals who have been struggling valiantly to combat the problem. For another, the search has taught us a great deal about the depth and complexity of the problem of violence in schools and hopefully has pointed us toward more effective responses.

We've learned that violence problems in schools have

taken decades to develop; therefore we mustn't expect any single person, policy, program, committee, or strategy to quickly solve them. We've also learned that every individual—adult and child alike—has been affected in some way by violence in school, either through personal experience or by living or working with people whose misguided beliefs, feelings, attitudes, and behaviors concerning violence make them part of the problem instead of the solution. We've learned that violence in schools has a far reaching effect that goes beyond individuals to affect entire school systems in ways that render them ineffective for solving the violence problem.

In other words, we've learned the all-important lesson that violence problems are *systemic* and that it will take a *systematic* effort to deal effectively with them. It takes a system to crack a system. Before we discuss Johnson Institute's systematic approach to solving violence problems in schools, let's take a closer look at some of the roots of the problem.

A Closer Look at Violence in Schools: Entitlement and Tolerance

From Johnson Institute's extensive and thorough research on the problem of violence in schools, a very important and critical discovery was made. In spite of all the theoretical debates on the causes, and in spite of all the resulting programs and strategies that have been developed to solve the problem, violent behavior in schools is increasing because of two pervasive attitudes: *entitlement* and *tolerance.*

Many students feel *entitled* to act violently toward teachers and toward other students, especially passive, weaker, or younger ones. Their lack of sensitivity toward the effect violence has on others inclines many students to think it's perfectly normal and acceptable to express their anger, get their needs met, or fulfill their desires in violent ways. This sense of entitlement to act in violent ways is not being addressed effectively by adults in the schools. In fact, it is being *tolerated* by them. Students by and large ignore adults' warnings regarding violent behavior because adults usually tolerate the behavior and allow students to get away with it.

Many responsible adults in schools (administrators, teachers, student service workers, coaches) are unwittingly playing a large role in the escalation of youth violence by means of their enabling behaviors. And the sum of those "enabling" behaviors is the attitude of tolerance. Because students' violent behaviors evoke such fear in educators, many shut their eyes before, during, and often after violent incidents, usually rationalizing that "as long as it does not involve them personally, it is not their job to do anything about it." As Dr. Prothrow-Stith points out, "Teachers and school administrators often know what is going on, but feel powerless to halt the process leading up to a fight."[5] *

Another highly respected expert, Dan Olweus, a professor at the University of Bergen in Norway, who conducted a 20-year study on bully/victim violence in Scandinavian schools, concurs: "Teachers do. . . relatively little to put a stop to bullying at school, according to both the bullied and bullying students."[6]

Besides feeling powerless to stop violent interactions among students, many teachers, as well as other school professionals, often justify the violent interactions among students as "something all children have to endure as part of growing up." When teachers see violent behavior but do nothing to intervene or stop it (tolerance), the natural result is for students to think it is their right to act that way (entitlement) because adults, by their inaction, appear to sanction such behavior.

It is important to note that many students also tolerate violent behavior by their peers for fear of retaliation or rejection, or because they get caught up in the sense of power violence can bring. Even so, it is adult tolerance of violence that contributes most significantly to the problem. Any response by schools must involve a direct and unequivocal confrontation of both entitlement and tolerance. (More on this subject will come later in this booklet.)

---

*To learn more about enabling violence problems in schools, read *Violence in Schools: The Enabling Factor* (Minneapolis: Johnson Institute, 1994.)

In addition to the attitudes of entitlement and tolerance, we also discovered another factor that can seriously hamper schools' abilities to solve violence problems. Surprisingly, it is the lack of a clear, all-encompassing, and universally acceptable definition of violence—one that all students and educators can understand, accept, and use to identify or recognize violent incidents when they occur or when they are about to occur.

A Working Definition of Violence for Schools

Violence is hard to define. It can exist anywhere along a continuum from what appears to be a somewhat benign action like jumping in front of someone who is already in line at the ticket counter, to the Holocaust of World War II. Even the dictionary has five separate entries for the word violence that leave the term open to many levels of interpretation. Society's ambivalence toward violence also confuses the issue. For example, most people are angered when they see one person deliberately and violently knock another person down on the sidewalk. Yet, at football games, we actually cheer when people are knocked down with deliberate and unnecessary roughness. This is just one example of how we often rationalize certain acts of violence as "sport" or "entertainment."

Violence is a diffuse problem, appearing in many different forms and with many different interpretations. That is why schools need to first clearly define what they mean by "violence" before educators can focus directly and act directly on those forms of violence that occur within the perimeters and boundaries of their individual campuses. Once violence is clearly defined so that boundaries are set and there is no room for ambivalence or individual interpretation of violent incidents, then educators can begin to use the definition as a tool for intervention and prevention and for clarifying for students what behavior is unacceptable.

Generally speaking, we can say that violence occurs

whenever a person is exposed to negative actions on the part of one or more persons. Negative actions can be:

- *mean or hurtful words:* threats, put-downs, racial slurs, name calling, sarcasm, joking, teasing, taunting, ridiculing;

- *mean or hurtful looks:* demeaning facial expressions, eye-rolling, staring, sticking out the tongue, sexual "looks";

- *mean or hurtful signs:* nasty gestures, threatening with a fist or weapon, touching oneself or someone else in a sexual manner to cause embarrassment, exposing one's private parts;

- *mean or hurtful overt acts:* slapping, pinching, hitting, punching, shoving, pulling, poking, kicking, tripping, stomping, cutting, hair pulling, beating;

- *mean or hurtful covert acts:* ignoring or violating a person's wishes or rights, silent threats, ostracizing, isolating others, stepping in front of someone who is standing in line, manipulating friendships.

A simple working definition of violence for educators:

Violence occurs whenever anyone inflicts or threatens to inflict physical or emotional injury or discomfort upon another person's body, feelings, or possessions.

For students, the definition is simplified:

Violence is any mean word, look, sign, or act that hurts a person's body, feelings, or things.

It may seem unrealistic to use a definition of violence that includes what appears to be fairly normal or innocent adolescent behaviors like joking or teasing. The key lies in the potential these behaviors have for causing real emotional and physical injury. We have to start somewhere to change students'—and educators'—perceptions about violent behaviors if we are to succeed in solving the problem of violence in schools.

The most common form of violence in the school setting is *acquaintance violence*—incidents that happen between people who know each other (usually friends or classmates). An all too frequent form of acquaintance violence is the type that involves a perpetrator, or *bully*, and a victim. And, as you will see, if the goal of schools is to reduce and, in time, eliminate all incidents of violence from the school setting, then special emphasis must be placed on intervening with *bully/victim* violence.

Why Schools Should Focus on Bully/Victim Violence

There are, of course, many normal kinds of conflict situations that occur in school between students and between students and teachers: arguments about borrowed or damaged books or sneakers; arguments over girlfriends or boyfriends, arguments over rumors; coming late to class; unfair grades; late homework assignments; the list is endless. For most students, these normal conflicts with peers or teachers, although having the potential to escalate into violent incidents, lend themselves well to anger management, conflict resolution, and peer mediation skills. Many schools already provide training in these skills for students as a violence-prevention measure.

Such prevention measures, however, could be vastly improved if schools clearly defined what they meant by "violence" (any mean look, sign, or act that hurts a person's body, feelings, or things) and by making it clear that such behaviors are unacceptable and won't be tolerated. By doing this, schools give students—and teachers—a level playing field, with a clear set of rules or guidelines that will help them work out normal kinds of conflict situations without resorting to violence.

The type of conflict that occurs between bullies and their victims, however, is not related to normal disagreements, and it almost always involves violence. Here is a definition of bully/victim violence:

Bully/victim violence occurs whenever anyone intentionally, repeatedly, and over time inflicts or threatens to inflict physical or emotional injury or discomfort upon another person's body, feelings, or possessions.

In addition to the repetitive pattern of violence, what makes bully/victim violence different from violence that stems from a student's inability to resolve conflicts nonviolently or to manage his or her anger is that bully/victim violence *involves an imbalance of power and strength*. It almost never involves conflicts or quarrels between two people of approximately the same size or physical or emotional strength. In bully/victim violence, the victim feels helpless to adequately defend himself or herself against the bully. Bully/victim violence is not a careless, isolated act, but is intentional, often premeditated, and repeated over time. This type of violence happens regularly in schools.

Bully/victim violence has a distinct pattern that most people recognize and are upset by, but that few students or adults will try to intervene with. Why? Because bullies enjoy being violent and those who witness their actions are often too scared to confront them about it. "Bullies need to assert their power by subduing their victims, and show little empathy for their victims," writes Olweus. "They are usually very defiant and aggressive toward adults (including teachers and parents), often frightening them. Moreover, they are skilled at intimidating other students, as well as inducing them to become followers."[7]

Johnson Institute's *StudentView®* Survey indicates that a fairly well-defined group of students is involved repeatedly in starting physical fights or beating people up. Slightly over 4 percent of girls and nearly 14 percent of boys are involved in beating people up or starting fights three or more times a year. These students are most likely to be the school bullies. Because a certain number of girls who demonstrate bully tendencies are more likely to use verbal attacks and/or social exclusion as their preferred form of bullying behavior, this percentage may underrepresent the actual number of girl bullies. The *StudentView®* survey also shows that the percentage of students starting three or more fights a year peaks at about seventh grade for boys (with 15.8 percent starting three or more fights) and at about eighth grade for girls (with 5.5 percent starting three or more fights).

Bullies are not interested in learning anger management or conflict resolution skills because they derive a certain pleasure and sense of power from what they are doing. Bullies are not interested in resolving disputes or handling their anger. Likewise, bully/victim situations are not amenable to nor can they be resolved through peer mediation. Although bully/victim violence almost always requires adults' intervention, such intervention rarely occurs. Consequently, this type of violence is increasingly common in schools. It is actually spawned and sustained by entitlement and tolerance.

When a bully feels entitled to be violent toward others and the behavior is tolerated by adults as well as peers, the bully begins to believe that he or she enjoys a kind of sanctioned power over others in the school. The bully's power is also acknowledged and respected by other students—and sadly, by many educators—while at the same time being hated and feared.

Though many people believe gang members are primarily responsible for bullying at school, this is a misconception. The gang-related violence usually occurs between students or groups of students of perceived equal strength, and happens for different reasons than bullying—for example, power struggles, territorial transgressions, and the like. Gang violence is also a community and police problem that usually involves illegal activities that should be dealt with by the judicial system—not the schools.

Bully/victim violence has a "spreading effect." The tolerance of bully/victim violence in a school makes victims of everyone and creates more enablers than other types of violence. Moreover, it often incites other students, who might not otherwise act in violent ways, to become violent because they perceive tolerance as *permission* to be violent.

Bully/victim violence almost always requires adult intervention because it is power-driven, intentional, often premeditated, and repeats itself over time. When educators focus their efforts first and foremost on bully/victim acts of violence, they can act more effectively to reduce and, in time, eliminate other incidents of violence in their schools. Why? Because the way in which the problem of violence is *formulated* and *presented* to a school—to administrators, students, teachers, and parents—has an important impact on their readiness to do something about it.

There are several advantages in casting the problem of violence in schools in terms of bully/victim violence. By conceptualizing violence this way, the unacceptable, inappropriate, aggressive, destructive, and hurtful behavior of certain students (bullies) is anchored in a clear social context, and the painful mistreatment of the recipients of violent behavior (victims) also comes into clear focus. In this way, the repeated humiliation and suffering of the victims are brought into the foreground. This serves an important function of justifying the need for a systematic violence prevention and intervention program; the goal of stopping bullies is legitimized by the need to relieve the suffering of victims. Also, by focusing on the bully/victim problem in schools as a primary target for intervention, it is much easier to reach consensus among teachers, students, and parents that such problems must not be tolerated in their schools.

The adults, in particular, will be much more willing to take ownership of the problem and to accept that it is primarily their responsibility to intervene when they fully accept that psychologically stronger and more aggressive students must not be allowed to harass, threaten, humiliate, and hurt weaker and more defenseless students. It is much harder to get consensus for a violence prevention program that focuses on a less provocative and diffuse concept of violence. Moreover, such programs are likely to be unfocused and quickly degenerate into half-hearted, piecemeal attempts that won't work.

Finally, focusing on bully/victim violence as a primary target has beneficial effects for the schools in terms of reducing other forms of violent behavior and antisocial or conduct disorder behaviors, such as vandalism, truancy, theft, and alcohol or other drug abuse. As Olweus's research shows, intervention and prevention programs focused on bully/victim violence "serve to generally improve all students' satisfaction with school life, as well as classroom discipline."[8]

Most violence in schools stems from normal conflicts among students that go unresolved or quickly escalate into violence, and from acts of bullying. Because both types of violence are deeply entrenched problems that affect the whole school system, solving the problems will require a systemwide approach.

Why We Need a Systematic Approach to Solving Violence Problems

We have learned that violence is a systemic problem that can invade, pervade, and render whole systems dysfunctional—family systems, school systems, workplace systems, and other systems. With particular regard to school systems, we know that as violence problems grow in frequency and intensity, most staff members, including administrators, develop certain defenses: *denying* ("We don't have a problem here."); *rationalizing* ("What those boys did to those girls wasn't right, but boys will be boys."); *justifying* ("Our problem isn't violence, it's not enough staff."); *blaming* ("If the police would do their job, we wouldn't have a problem."); *minimizing* ("We have a few problems, but not like the senior high."); and *avoiding* ("It's not our responsibility, it's the principal's."). We also know that as violence problems in schools grow in intensity and frequency, most students develop similar *defenses*: blaming, withdrawing, keeping secrets, and stuffing feelings of anger, frustration, fear, guilt, or shame. In cases of bully/victim violence, the victims often develop feelings of being flawed or of deserving such treatment, especially when no one intervenes to help them.

Violence problems affect schools, families, and the workplace in many of the same ways other systemic problems such as alcohol and other drug abuse do. But when the problem is alcohol or other drug abuse, rarely is anyone motivated to do anything about the problem. They work instead to keep the problem covered up. Only a pattern of recurring and increasingly painful or disruptive crises will move a family, school, or workplace inexorably to the point where something must be done.

This is where today's problem of violence in schools is different from other systemic problems; many students and adults are highly motivated by fear to do something about it. Students are waiting for adults to become responsible and take control of the school environment. Many adults who work in schools are afraid of the violence, too, and want to do something about it. They simply need to be shown how much power they have to transform a violence-prone school environment into a safe, supportive, and nurturing learning atmosphere where both adults and children feel protected and respected. And they need a comprehensive strategy for doing it.

Johnson Institute's approach to solving violence problems in schools is predicated on the democratic principle that, while at school, every child has the right to be free of oppression and repeated, intentional hurt and humiliation. In short, every child has the right to feel respected and protected in school. It is the responsibility of those adults who work for and within the school to protect those rights and to establish and enforce policies that require everyone within the school to respect those rights. To that end, Johnson Institute has developed the comprehensive and systematic *Respect and Protect* approach for solving violence problems that:

- is both adult-centered and student-centered;

- contains both a prevention element (*environmental control*) and an intervention element (*choices, consequences, and contracts*);

- is based on the principle that everyone has an obligation to respect and protect the rights of others; and

- promotes a systemwide school ethos that states in effect: **"Violence is not okay. We do not tolerate it here."**

Because violence has become a systemic problem in schools, it requires a systematic approach to solve it. When solving alcohol and other drug problems in family, school, or work systems, we must deal with the chemical dependents and their codependents, and dismantle the "enabling system" that spawns and supports the destructive use of chemicals. Likewise, in solving violence problems we must deal with the perpetrators and victims of violence, and dismantle the enabling system that supports and spawns the violence.

The four goals of Johnson Institute's *Respect and Protect* approach to violence prevention and intervention are:

1. To ensure the safety and well-being of both students and educators.

2. To reduce the severity and frequency of, and eventually eliminate, all incidents of violence from the school setting.

3. To eliminate the two pervasive attitudes that directly spawn and support violence in schools: entitlement and tolerance.

4. To create a safe, supportive, nurturing, nonpunitive atmosphere highly conducive to learning.

The *Respect and Protect* approach is not a militant, punitive, "get rid of the enemy" type of strategy. Instead, it requires that all adults within the school take responsibility to create and maintain a total school environment that is safe, secure, supportive, and nurturing, but that does not tolerate violence in any form. This is *environmental control*. But environmental control is not the same thing as "controlling the environment," which usually involves using militant kinds of security measures to keep students in line. Instead, it is creating a school environment that supports adult efforts to intervene in—not ignore—violence when they see it. It also involves policies, programs, and educational approaches that support nonviolent resolution of conflicts and a systematic approach using *choices, consequences, and contracts* to address problems of bullying and other types of violence.

In some schools, especially those in which weapons or gangs are prevalent, a more militant approach may be necessary at first. But such approaches provide only short-term solutions. When a militant or punitive approach is maintained over time, it often transforms the learning environment into a prison-like or military encampment atmosphere. Students and teachers may feel safer as long as police, security guards, or other measures are in place, but the atmosphere is still not conducive to learning. Moreover, violence is not really dispelled by a "security system," but merely driven underground or outside to playgrounds, school buses, or routes to and from school where students and teachers are still vulnerable.

The Johnson Institute believes that children must be taught by responsible adults, that no one is entitled to use violence to express anger, resolve conflicts, or for any other reason, and that violence will not be tolerated. We believe that the key to preventing violence lies in shaping children's beliefs, attitudes, and behaviors before violence becomes their automatic answer to expressing angry or aggressive feelings, resolving conflicts, or simply as a way to get what they want. This is what the adult-centered prevention element called *environmental control* is meant to achieve.

Environmental control is actually achieved by a change in adult beliefs, attitudes, and behavior toward violence. It is simply the collective and determined stance of responsible adults in a school to eliminate the attitudes of "entitlement" and "tolerance." This is accomplished when all the adults in a school collectively agree to act in a concerted, decisive, and consistent way to prevent or intervene with any student who is threatening to use or is using violence, especially bully/victim violence, according to the definitions given earlier (see pages 17 and 20).

The environmental control element of the *Respect and Protect* approach is based in part on Olweus' 20-year research on bully/victim violence in schools in Norway. According to Olweus, bully/victim violence is a growing problem in schools in all societies, and at all grade levels. Olweus developed a core program for dealing with bully/victim violence that consists of a set of routine rules and strategies of communication and action for dealing with present and future bullying problems. The core program involves specific measures taken by adults on three different levels:

- *Measures at the school level:*

  — Student/teacher survey on prevalence of bullying

  — School conference day

  — Better adult supervision during recess and lunch time

— Meeting between staff and parents (PTA meeting) on bullying policies

- *Measures at the class level:*

— Class rules against bullying

— Regular class meetings to discuss programs

- *Measures at the individual level:*

— Serious talks with bullies and victims

— Serious talks with parents of involved students

— Teachers and parents creatively working together to identify and impose nonpunitive consequences for violent behavior.

Although the whole-school policy approach that the Olweus model promotes is based on adults taking action to stop bully/victim violence, the consequences or measures taken on all three levels are fairly informal and unstructured. Sanctions imposed on bullies are at the discretion of individual teachers. Moreover, the model is directed only at bully/victim violence, not at all incidents of violence. Nevertheless, the consistent action of concerned and committed adults is the key ingredient, as the outcome data has shown.

In Johnson Institute's *Respect and Protect* approach, the environmental control element works to prevent all incidents of violence. When other students in the school see that any incident of violence is immediately addressed by adults, that specific measures are brought to bear on the perpetrator (bully) or other students involved, that a clear onus is placed on the violent behavior instead of empowerment to repeat it, these students receive a powerful message. Under this kind of consistent and ongoing adult action over time, bullies lose their prestige and power among other students. Moreover, because of the shared school ethos, all students—and adults—are forced to look at and change their own inclinations to violent behavior.

The environmental control element is a nonmilitant, nonpunitive, and effective strategy for eliminating violence as a value throughout the school. The element of adult-centered environmental control permeates the school system with an aura of nontolerance of any kind of violence by anyone—student or adult—anywhere, at any time. It is especially the collective, determined, and consistent underscoring of the value of nontolerance by adults that seems to act as a force for good—causing students in general to integrate that value into their own behavior. It is the willingness of adults, not only to intervene and to enforce the value, but to integrate it into their own actions and words that creates such a powerful impression on students.

Peter Steinglass, M.D., a psychiatrist and head of the prestigious Adler Institute in New York, discovered the same principle at work in his now famous 10-year study of the effect of alcoholism on families.[9] According to Steinglass, the difference between families that seem to transfer or pass on alcoholism to their children, at least in terms of behavior, and those that seem to prevent alcoholism from being transferred to the next generation is that in the latter group, the adults act in a very determined way to prevent alcoholism from becoming an accepted "norm." While no one but the alcoholic can change his or her behavior, adults in families that prevent alcoholism from moving into the next generation do not allow the alcoholic family member (when he or she is drinking or drunk) to participate in, infringe upon, or disrupt family rituals, routines, and regulatory behaviors. In other words, Grandpa is not allowed to come to the family Christmas party drunk and no one in the family is forced to pretend that Grandpa does not have a problem. These adults make it quite clear to children why Grandpa cannot come. Children in such families get a very strong message that being drunk is not okay and will not be tolerated.

The "determined stance" of adults in such families actually serves as an extremely effective prophylactic that appears to prevent children from mimicking a dysfunctional behavior. When children see the "collective and determined stance" of adults in the school not to tolerate violence, they learn that in order to "belong" they cannot engage in violent behavior of any kind.

It is interesting to note that Steinglass's study also found that children from families in which adults take a determined stance not to tolerate alcoholic behavior do not have a tendency as adults to marry into other alcoholic families—an otherwise common and predictable behavior among adult children of alcoholics. These children, too, become intolerant of intolerable behavior caused by alcoholism, and appear to break the cycle of family alcoholism. There is good reason to believe that students who are taught "intolerance" and "nonentitlement" to violent behavior by determined adult educators will not perpetuate it in their school systems. The exception may be those "bullies" who have a pathologic involvement with violence and therefore may be incapable of unlearning or changing this behavior.

Although the prevention element of adult-centered environmental control is a critical and necessary part of any approach to solving violence problems in schools, Johnson Institute believes that a second, and equally important, element is required: a highly structured intervention process that is student-centered. Even though the adult-centered, whole-school policy approach of Olweus has proved successful in other countries, such as Sweden, his research has been concentrated in countries with more homogenous populations than the United States. Moreover, the model is directed at only one very specific form of violence—bully/victim incidents.

In the United States, because of our heterogeneous population and the diverse social pressures it creates, the problem of violence in our schools is far more complex and requires a more comprehensive approach.

Although using the one element of adult-centered environmental control might be sufficient for some schools, particularly at the elementary level, for middle schools and junior and senior high schools, a much more comprehensive and systematic approach is called for. That is why Johnson Institute's *Respect and Protect* approach introduces a second element—choices, consequences, and contracts—a student-centered intervention process that provides a formal structure of graduated levels of sanctions geared to the frequency and severity of students' involvement in violent incidents. The choices, consequences, and contracts intervention element is a supportive and nurturing process that seeks to facilitate behavioral change in all students who engage in or are victims of violent behavior. The process gives educators an extremely effective tool for dealing immediately, effectively, and in a very humanitarian way with all incidents of violence—bully/victim violence as well as violent incidents that result from normal conflict situations.

The structured intervention element of the *Respect and Protect* approach uses a combination of logical consequences for behavior, contracts spelling out what the consequences will be if the behavior happens again, restitution, and education. For any incident of violence, the choices, consequences, and contracts intervention element:

- defines what actions or activities school staff need to carry out;

- identifies a specific type of behavior contract to be used to identify what the consequences will be if the students do act out in violent behavior again; and

- provides clear guidelines for appropriate consequences for the current behavior.

The structured intervention element also differentiates between violence that results from normal conflict situations and that related to bullying. When the violence results from a normal conflict situation, both students involved are given a chance to resolve it using conflict resolution skills or peer mediation. They are required to complete a life-skills exercise to help them learn conflict resolution and anger management skills they can use in the future. They are also given a no-violence contract. When a situation is identified as bully/victim violence, the student who is doing the bullying is placed on a contract, given consequences such as restitution and limitations on activities, and referred to a corrective support group. The victims, too, are referred to a support group to help them learn life skills that empower them to protect and assert themselves effectively and nonviolently, and that reduce the likelihood of future victimization.

Students who continue to break the no-violence rule move on to higher levels of consequences and more intense intervention efforts, such as being assigned to attend a weekly corrective support group or, if a behavior disorder is suspected, being referred for psychosocial evaluation. The choices, consequences, and contracts intervention element uses a graduated approach to intervention so that a particular student's second or third offense has greater consequences than his or her first offense. The intervention element also involves a centralized reporting mechanism. All too often, a student will be "caught" fighting in one class or by one teacher and pay the consequence, only to do something similar in another class or setting. What appears to each teacher as isolated incidents may in fact be a pattern of violent behavior that needs to be addressed. Without a centralized reporting system, the student's "pattern of violent behavior" is never effectively dealt with.

Centralized reporting of incidents is integral to the structured intervention of choices, consequences, and contracts. Whenever a teacher or other staff member intervenes in either a conflict situation or a bully/victim incident, he or she fills out a brief form describing the incident and what he or she did to intervene. The reports are then sent to a designated staff member (or a team), for example, the principal or the Student Assistance Program (SAP) coordinator. That person then has the opportunity to identify students who are developing patterns of repeated violent behavior—or ongoing victimization.

The purpose of the structured intervention element is to provide schools with an efficient tool for sorting out and dealing appropriately and fairly with individual students engaged in different levels of violence. It is a systematic process for determining over time the degree, frequency, and severity of a student's violent behavior. When a pattern of violent behavior is identified, the student undergoes a specific protocol of rehabilitative education and support that gives him or her an opportunity to change the unacceptable behavior.

It is strongly recommended that all schools formally incorporate anger management, conflict resolution, and peer mediation skill training for students into their curriculum. But even in schools where this information is not formally included in the curriculum, it can be informally presented by the examples teachers and other staff set on a daily basis. It is also recommended that workshops or in-service training be provided to all teachers and other staff to help them examine how their own enabling behaviors (misguided beliefs, feelings, attitudes, and behaviors concerning violence) can contribute to the problem. In addition, staff need skills training in the use of intervention and prevention techniques for dealing with violent incidents resulting from both normal conflict situations and from bullying.*

It is important to note that the structured intervention element of choices, consequences, and contracts is not an appropriate tool for dealing with the problem of gangs or weapons. Schools need special help to deal effectively with these problems because the type of violence created by the presence of gangs and weapons is different from normal conflicts or common bullying—gang violence or weapon violence are criminal issues. Whenever guns or other weapons are brought to school, whether they are used or just "shown off," the school's policy regarding weapons should always take precedence over whatever policies are established for addressing violence stemming from normal conflict or bullying.

---

* For more information about available training on Johnson Institute's systematic approach to violence prevention (The *Respect and Protect* Program), call Johnson Institute at 1-800-231-5165.

Gangs and weapons are community and police problems and every effort should be made to avoid turning the school into an arm of the juvenile justice system. To that end, the school's policy should be that whenever a student is found in possession of a weapon, the school should confiscate the weapon, hold the student until the police and the student's parents arrive, and turn the matter over to the judicial system. Severe disciplinary actions, such as suspension or expulsion, must be used to reinforce the school's message that violence will not be tolerated. Educators must remain educators and not become police or turn their schools into police states.

An excellent way for schools to avoid criminalizing *all* incidents of violence is to integrate the *Respect and Protect* approach as part of an overall Student Assistance Program (SAP). While the *Respect and Protect* approach can be successfully implemented in schools that do not have SAPs, the intervention element of the program works most efficiently and effectively when it is integrated as part of a school-based SAP. The student-centered intervention element of choices, consequences, and contracts, when placed under the auspices of a formal SAP program, adds credibility to the adult-centered element of environmental control as a means of creating a safe "controlled environment," free of the type of militant, punitive, or security-oriented atmosphere that only serves to drive violent behavior underground or outside the school. Moreover, integrating the *Respect and Protect* approach or placing it under the auspices of a Student Assistance Program enables the school to decriminalize violent behavior and to cast it as a behavioral health issue. When adult-centered prevention (environmental control) and student-centered intervention (choices, consequences and contracts) are combined with the highly organized and systematized problem-solving components of an SAP—education, identification, intervention, assessment, referral, and support—a school can have the most comprehensive, practical, effective, and inexpensive solution for solving violence problems that is currently available.

Let's look now at how using the *Respect and Protect* approach in conjunction with SAP can help solve violence problems in schools.

How SAPs Can Enhance the *Respect and Protect* Program

Educators and others often see violence as a single phenomenon requiring a single response. But violence affects different students in different ways. And these differing experiences imply different needs. No single program, policy, person, or strategy can be expected to solve violence problems. We need a multifaceted approach like *Respect and Protect,* in conjunction with an SAP, that recognizes the spectrum of needs of various target groups and that can develop appropriate policies, procedures, activities, and services based on those needs.

Any systemic problem within a school, including violence, can be most effectively addressed through the use of a student assistance program.* SAPs provide an already established continuum of services ideally organized and focused on addressing each element of a systemic problem. It is not a piecemeal or shotgun approach, but draws on all the problem-solving resources within a school and focuses them on manageable parts of the problem. The continuum of services SAP provides includes:

- preventive education for students, teachers, and community leaders;

- identification of problems;

- intervention with troubled students;

- referral of students to appropriate resources;

---

* To learn more about student assistance programming, read *When Chemicals Come to School, The Student Assistance Program Model.* (See the list of resources on page 47.)

- support groups providing graduated levels of support for different target groups of students;

- parent education and training; and

- community support.

Solving violence problems in conjunction with an SAP enables educators to cast violence problems (other than gangs and weapons) in the school as behavioral health issues, rather than as criminal or delinquency issues. This gives students and teachers the message that violent behavior is not "normal" or healthy, but unhealthy and abnormal, and something the whole school system needs to prevent.

Student assistance programming is also the most visible and viable way for a school system to change how it has been enabling the development and presence of violence problems (tolerance). It is the proper vehicle for dealing with the systemic problem of violence in schools, because it invites educators and students to examine the fact that in some degree a violence-prone school setting has become a dysfunctional school setting. In such schools, violence becomes the organizing principle around which the whole school system adapts its routines, rituals, and regulatory behaviors. Windows are barred and doors become barriers or check points with metal detectors. Students (and teachers) avoid restrooms, playgrounds, and sometimes even hallways. Students and educators pretend not to see what they see.

Just as a family that permits or tolerates a member's violent behavior to victimize other members is enabling the problem to continue or worsen, so, too, a school system that tolerates acts of violence against or by its students or staff is feeding and sustaining such violence. Schools must dismantle their enabling behaviors before the problem will get any better. This is not to say that schools cause or are in any way to blame for violence problems. It is merely to point out that schools must confront the issue of "enabling" as a contributing factor to the escalation of youth violence. The failure of educators to be actively involved in preventing and intervening in youthful acts of violence can, in some ways, be traced to their individual "patterns of enabling"—the patterns of what they think, feel, and do (or fail to think, feel, and do)—that helps support and sustain violence in schools.*

Finally, using an SAP program avoids the pitfall of having one person or official in the school designated as the "Violence Czar or Expert." The *Respect and Protect* approach, in conjunction with an SAP, is a team approach that invites and compels all adults in the school to facilitate the servicing of students' needs. Successful violence prevention is predicated unequivocally on collective adult action, involvement, commitment, and follow-through. An SAP-based *Respect and Protect* approach to violence problems also provides concrete and primary benefits for all students, staff, parents, and the whole community.

Although the Johnson Institute believes that the *Respect and Protect* approach works most effectively when integrated with a school's student assistance program, it is still possible for schools without formal SAPs to use this approach successfully to solve violence problems. With a centralized system for reporting and action, together with the active participation of *all* adults in the school—from the principal to the cafeteria workers—schools *can* create safe learning environments, free from the disruptive and fear-provoking effects of violence.

---

* To learn more about enabling behaviors that support violence in schools, read *Violence in Schools: The Enabling Factor* (Minneapolis: Johnson Institute, 1994)

Appendix

Where Does Your School System Stand on Violence Problems?

Knowing where your school stands in relation to violence problems is one of the first steps in addressing such problems. Use the questionnaire below to assess how well or how poorly your school system is currently dealing with violence. You may also use it as a pre- and post-program survey to demonstrate the change in a school system's perception of violence problems after implementing a formal violence-prevention program such as *Respect and Protect*.

Indicate your assessment by circling the appropriate number on the agree/disagree continuum.

	strongly disagree		neutral		strongly agree
1. On the whole, our board of education, administrators, staff, students, and parents openly acknowledge the scope of violence-related problems affecting students in the community.	1	2	3	4	5
2. There is agreement that our current strategies for solving violence related problems work successfully.	1	2	3	4	5
3. There is good cooperation among school staff members and between the school system and other segments of the community in solving violence problems.	1	2	3	4	5

	strongly disagree		neutral		strongly agree

4. All levels of the school system are aware of how violence has been affecting both children and adults within the system and understand the concepts of denial, tolerance, entitlement, enabling, and intervention.
   1 2 3 4 5

5. All levels of the school system are aware of the differing needs of students—those who engage in violent behaviors and those who are affected by the violent behaviors of bullies or of family violence.
   1 2 3 4 5

6. The school has been involved in significant violence-prevention education for students, staff, and parents.
   1 2 3 4 5

7. The school system does not feel responsible for causing the violence problem and does not blame the problem on other segments of the community (e.g., parents, the police).
   1 2 3 4 5

8. The staff feel adequate and competent to deal with violence problems in general, and with violent students in particular.
   1 2 3 4 5

9. The system does not fear being blamed for violence problems in the school by other segments of the community, by parents, or by neighboring school systems.
   1 2 3 4 5

	strongly disagree	neutral		strongly agree

10. Administrators, student-services staff, and teachers have examined their tendency to tolerate violent behavior by students and have corrected their enabling behaviors.   1 2 3 4 5

11. Procedural aspects of enabling have been examined and corrected. Clear policies governing violent behavior, gang activity, and possession of weapons have been developed and are enforced.   1 2 3 4 5

12. Most school professionals in the system have a good sense of how their own personal beliefs, attitudes, and behaviors can foster either violence problems or a safe, preventive atmosphere.   1 2 3 4 5

13. Changes have been made in policies, procedures, and services offered to students that help violence problems to be dealt with effectively.   1 2 3 4 5

14. Student violence is discussed openly and publicly within the system. Respect for privacy is not confused with secrecy.   1 2 3 4 5

15. Students and staff openly and constructively discuss beliefs, attitudes, feelings, and behaviors relating to violence problems in the school.   1 2 3 4 5

16. Staff members frequently intervene with students engaged in violent behavior in a caring but firm way.   1 2 3 4 5

	strongly disagree	neutral		strongly agree

17. School counselors are knowledgeable regarding violent behavior and routinely confront their students about it. 1 2 3 4 5

18. Staff members make efforts to confront negative and harmful beliefs, attitudes, and behaviors in one another that help support violence problems. 1 2 3 4 5

19. The school has developed close ties with police, parents, service organization, clergy, and others in the community to help resolve violence problems in school. 1 2 3 4 5

20. School professionals clearly understand the school system's present strengths and possibilities, as well as its limitations for dealing effectively with violence problems. 1 2 3 4 5

21. School staff frequently reassess goals and redefine limitations with respect to violence-prevention programming. 1 2 3 4 5

Add the 5 column scores to get an overall rating.

Total "1" responses _____ *x 1* = _____

Total "2" responses _____ *x 2* = _____

Total "3" responses _____ *x 3* = _____

Total "4" responses _____ *x 4* = _____

Total "5" responses _____ *x 5* = _____

TOTAL = _____

Ratings will range from a high total of 105 (all "Strongly Agree") to a low of 21 (all "Strongly Disagree").

Scores within the low range (21 to 48) indicate a perception that the school system lacks most of the characteristics of an effective response to student violence problems.

Scores in the middle range (49 to 76) indicate that a school system is making some definite attempts to deal effectively with student violence problems.

Low scores on individual survey items may indicate areas where improvement is needed. Scores in the high range indicate an effective and healthy system-wide response to student violence and other problems.

---

* This questionnaire is adapted from one appearing in *Solving Alcohol/Drug Problems in Your School: Why Student Assistace Programs Work* by Gary Anderson (Minneapolis: Johnson Institute, 1988).

Reference Notes

1. Deborah Prothrow-Stith and M. Weissman. 1991-1993. *Deadly Consequences: How Violence is Destroying Our Teenage Population and a Plan to Begin Solving the Problem.* New York: HarperPerennial, 162.

2. American Psychological Association. 1993. *Violence & Youth: Psychology's Response. Vol. I: Summary Report of the American Psychological Association Commission on Violence and Youth.* Washington, D.C.: APA, 19.

3. The results of this survey are based on the written answers of 65,193 sixth through twelfth graders who responded individually or as classes to a questionnaire printed in the April 23 to 25, 1993 issue of *USA Weekend* and in the *Classline Today* teaching plan, and distributed by the National Association of Secondary School Principals.

4. "Fighting a War on Weapons." *Education Week*, Dec. 8, 1993. As summarized in *Sunburst Update*, Winter 1994, 3.

5. Prothrow-Stith and Weismann, 1993, 175.

6. Dan Olweus, Ph.D. 1993. *Bullying at School: What We Know and What We Can Do.* Cambridge, Mass.: Blackwell Publishers, 20.

7. Olweus, 59.

8. Olweus, 113-114.

9. Peter Steinglass, et al. 1987. *The Alcoholic Family.* New York: Basic Books.